RUBANK BOOK OF FLUTE SOLOS
INTERMEDIATE LEVEL

MEDIA INCLUDED
Recordings
Accompaniments

PLAYBACK+
Speed • Pitch • Balance • Loop

CONTENTS

To access recordings and PDF accompaniments visit:
www.halleonard.com/mylibrary

Enter Code
8002-6182-1390-4016

ISBN 978-1-4950-6503-3

RUBANK®

HAL•LEONARD® CORPORATION
7777 W. BLUEMOUND RD. P.O. BOX 13819 MILWAUKEE, WI 53213

Visit Hal Leonard Online at
www.halleonard.com

Albumleaf

Flute

Richard Wagner
arranged by Adolf Hass

Con moto

Chanson Pastorale

Flute

Paul Koepke

Gavotta
From "Classical Symphony"

Flute

Serge Prokofieff
Transcribed by H. Voxman

Menuet

From "Platee"

J. P. Rameau
Transcribed by H. Voxman

Flute

Two Menuettos

From "Flute Sonata in C"

Flute

I

J. S. Bach
Edited by H. Voxman

II

Menuetto I da capo

8

Polovtsian Dance

From "Prince Igor"

Alexander Borodin
Arranged by Harold L. Walters

Flute

Slumber Song
(Schlummerlied, Op. 124, No. 16)

Flute

R. Schumann
Transcribed by R. Hervig

Canzona

Flute

Ferdinando Bertoni
Arranged by Aldolf Hass

Song Of India

From The Opera "Sadko"

Flute

N. Rimsky-Korsakow
Arranged by Henry W. Davis

Villanella

Flute

Paul Koepke

Flute

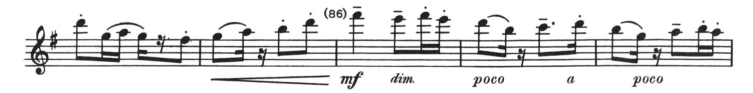

Menuetto

From "Eine Kleine Nachtmusik"

Flute

W. A. Mozart
Transcribed by H. Voxman